Night and Light

by Becca Heddle

OXFORD
UNIVERSITY PRESS

It gets dark at night.
What happens then?

I go to bed.

The chickens run into the coop.
They will be secure all night.

Owls perch up high.
They can see in the dark.
They hoot.

Bats dart when they hear bugs.

Bats are good at hearing.
They zoom to get bugs for dinner.

A light lures moths to it.

Foxes bark in the woods.

A pair of foxes look for food.

Foxes curl up when it gets light.
fox cub
My dog gets up.

The sun is up.
Rabbits hop into the air.
They dig in the soil.

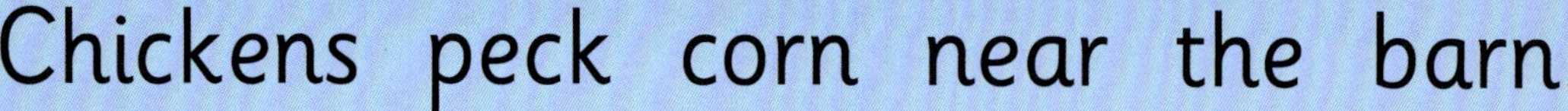

Chickens peck corn near the barn.

Lots of animals are alert in the light.

I feel good in the summer light.

The sun is low again.
When it gets dark ...
the night animals get up again.

I need to go to bed now. Good night!

Night animals

Light animals

Talk about which animals are awake at night and which animals are awake in the day.